Easy Interior

An Adult Coloring Book

Copyright © 2021Robber Fickle
All Rights Reserved.

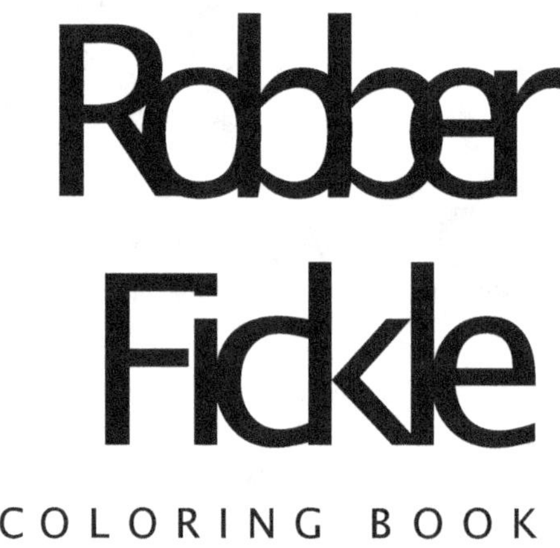

For Any Question and Suggestions
robberfickle@gmail.com

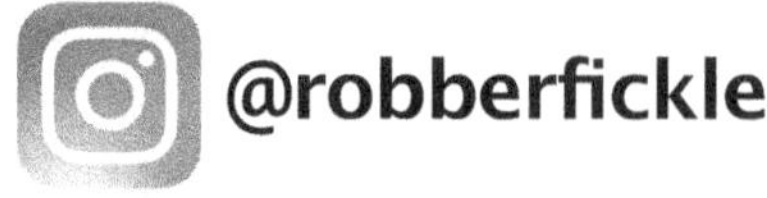

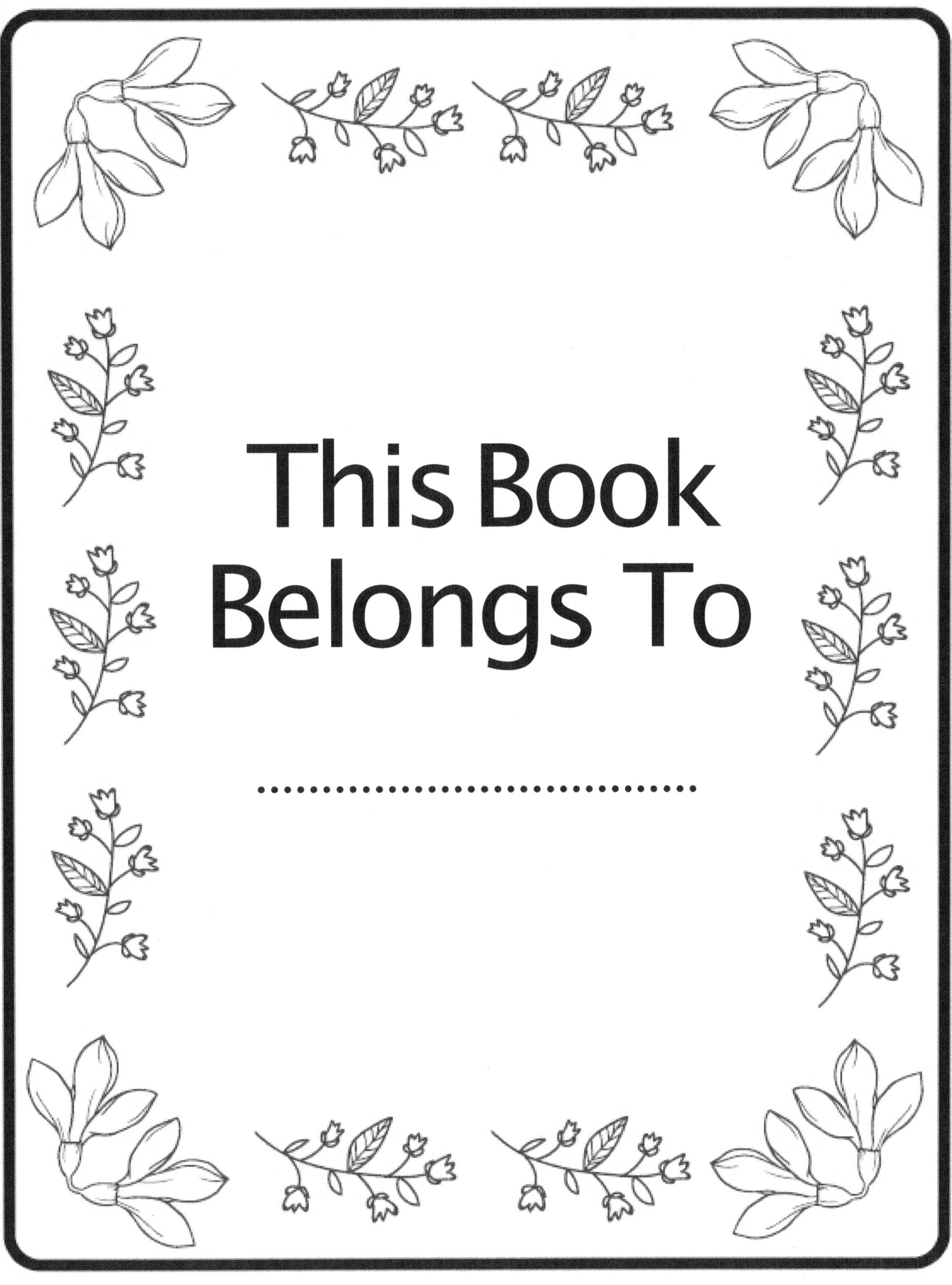

This Book Belongs To

....

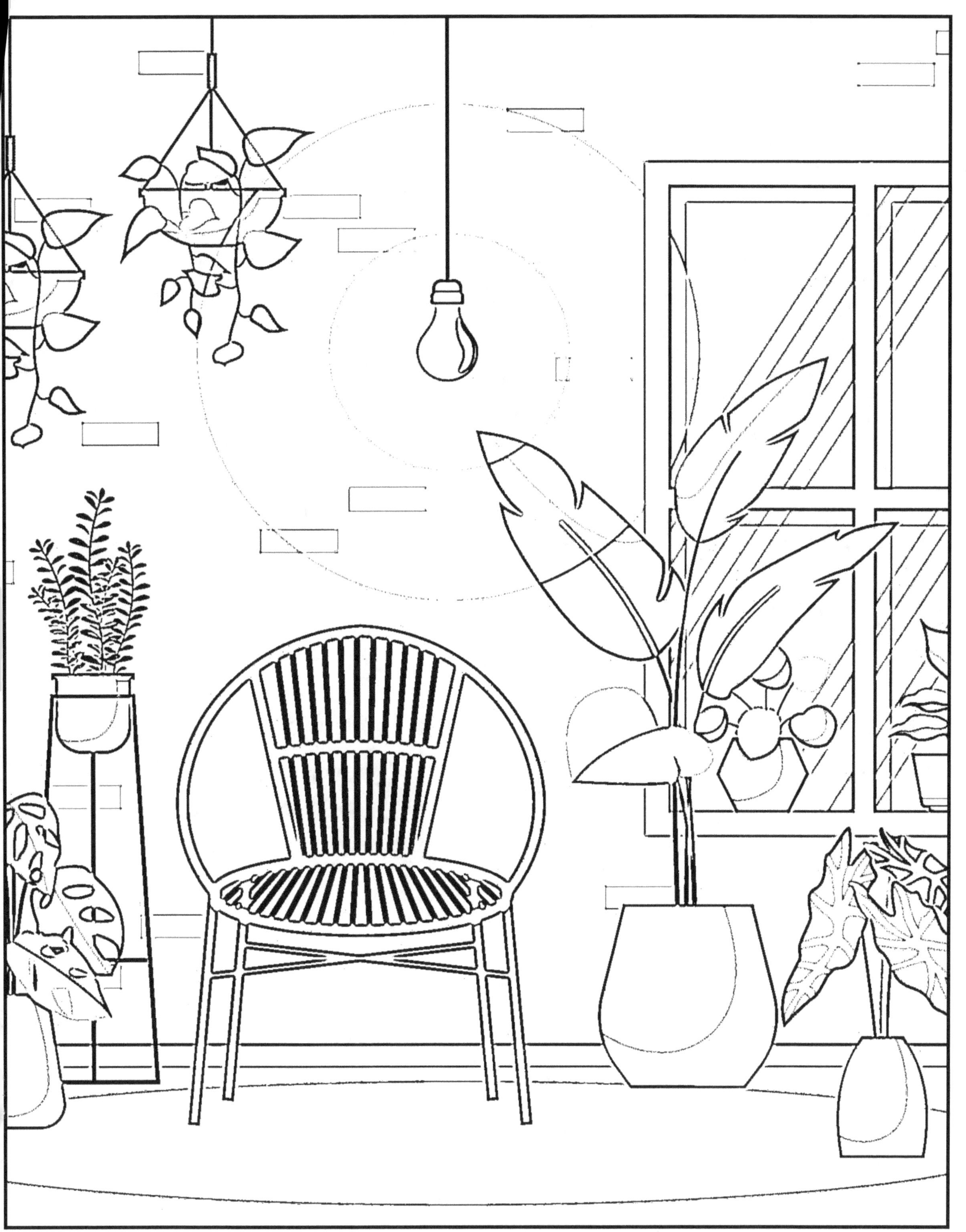

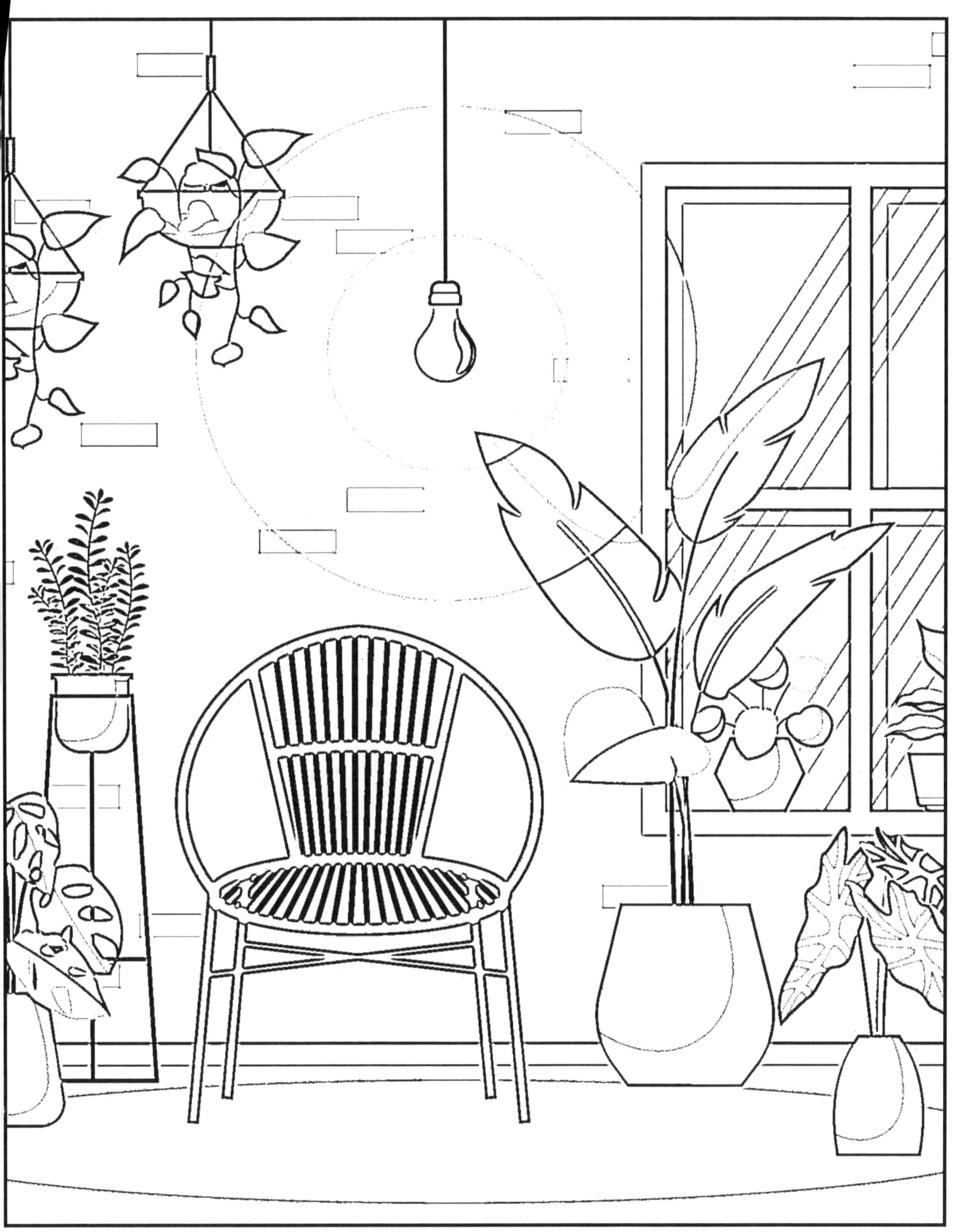

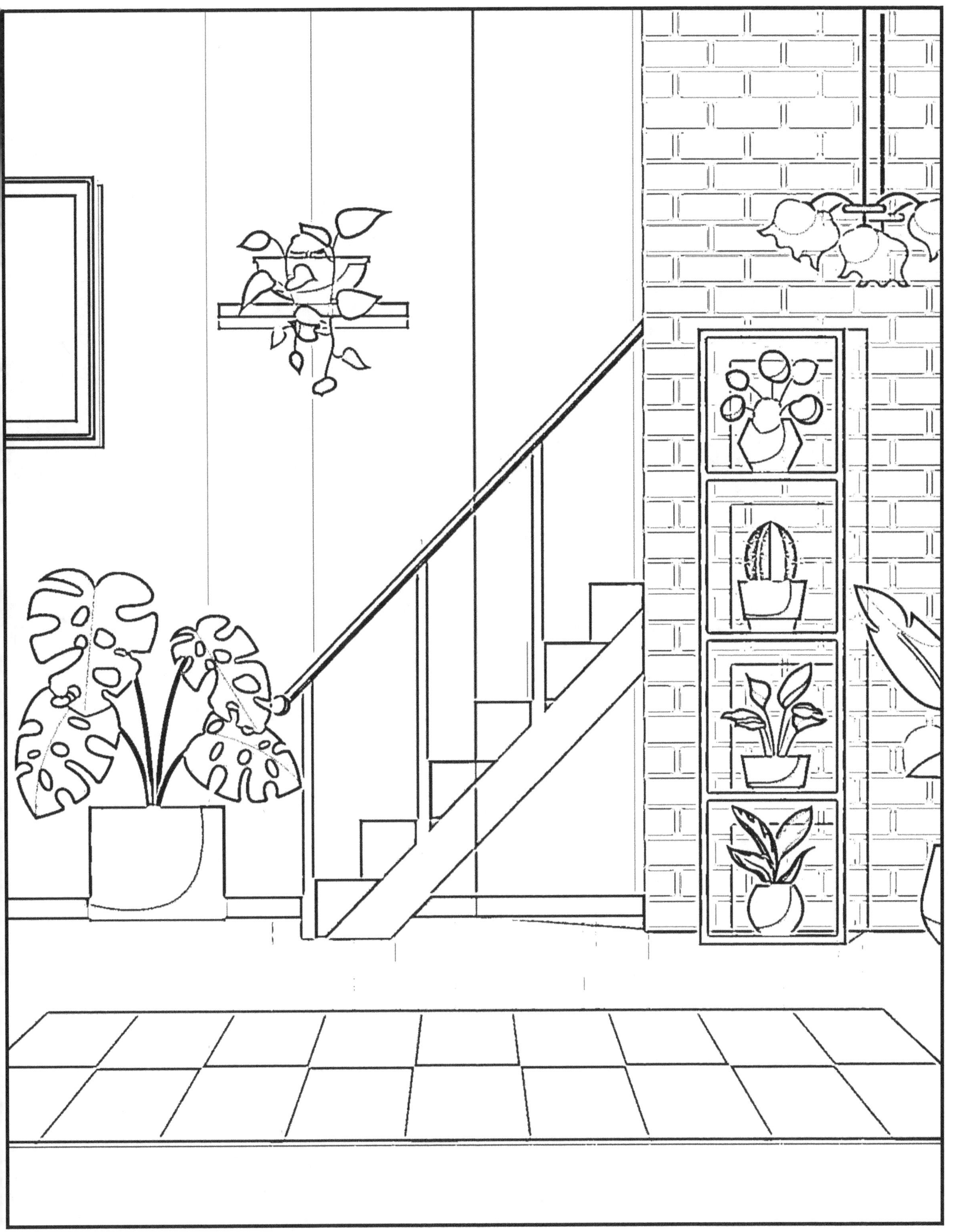

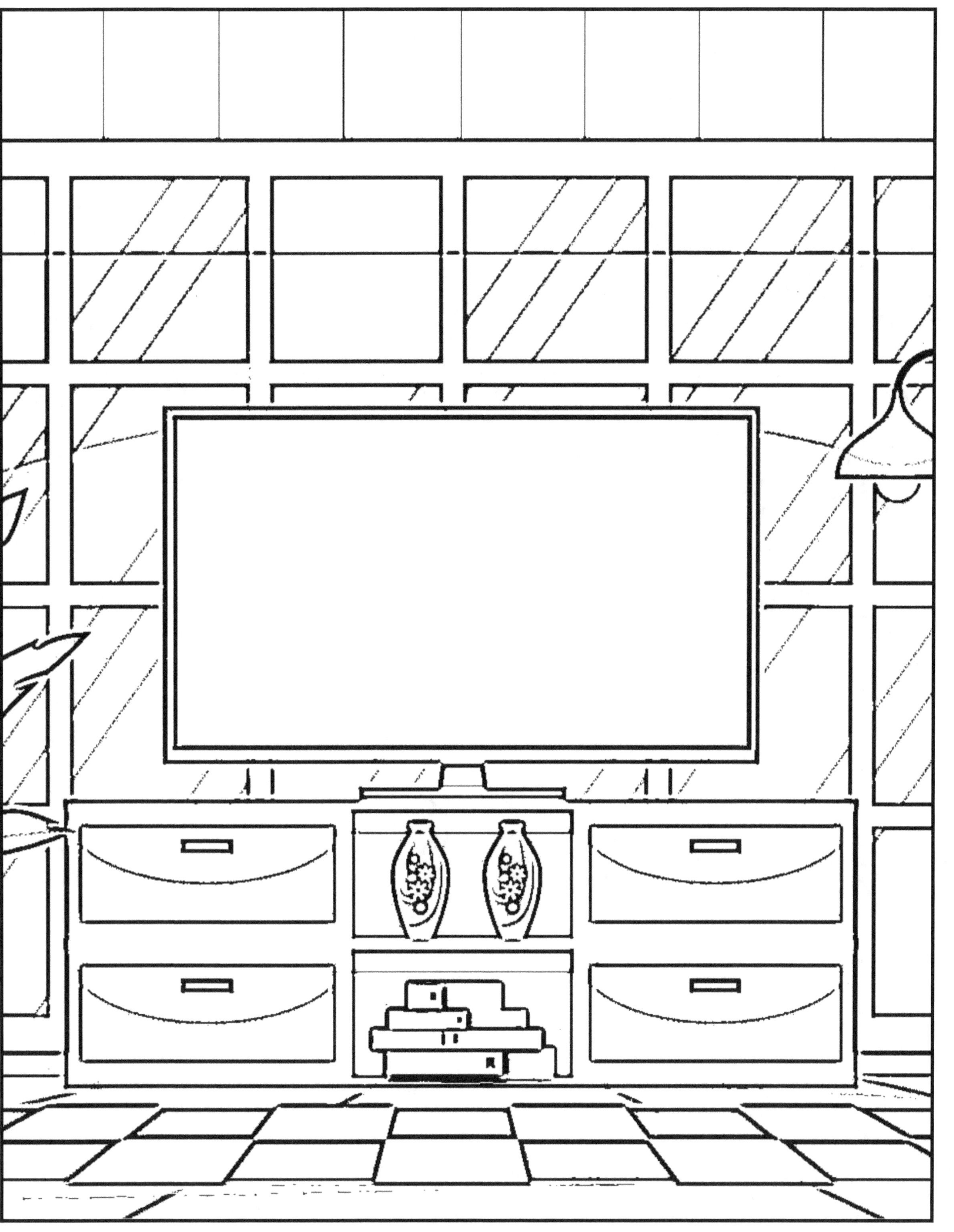

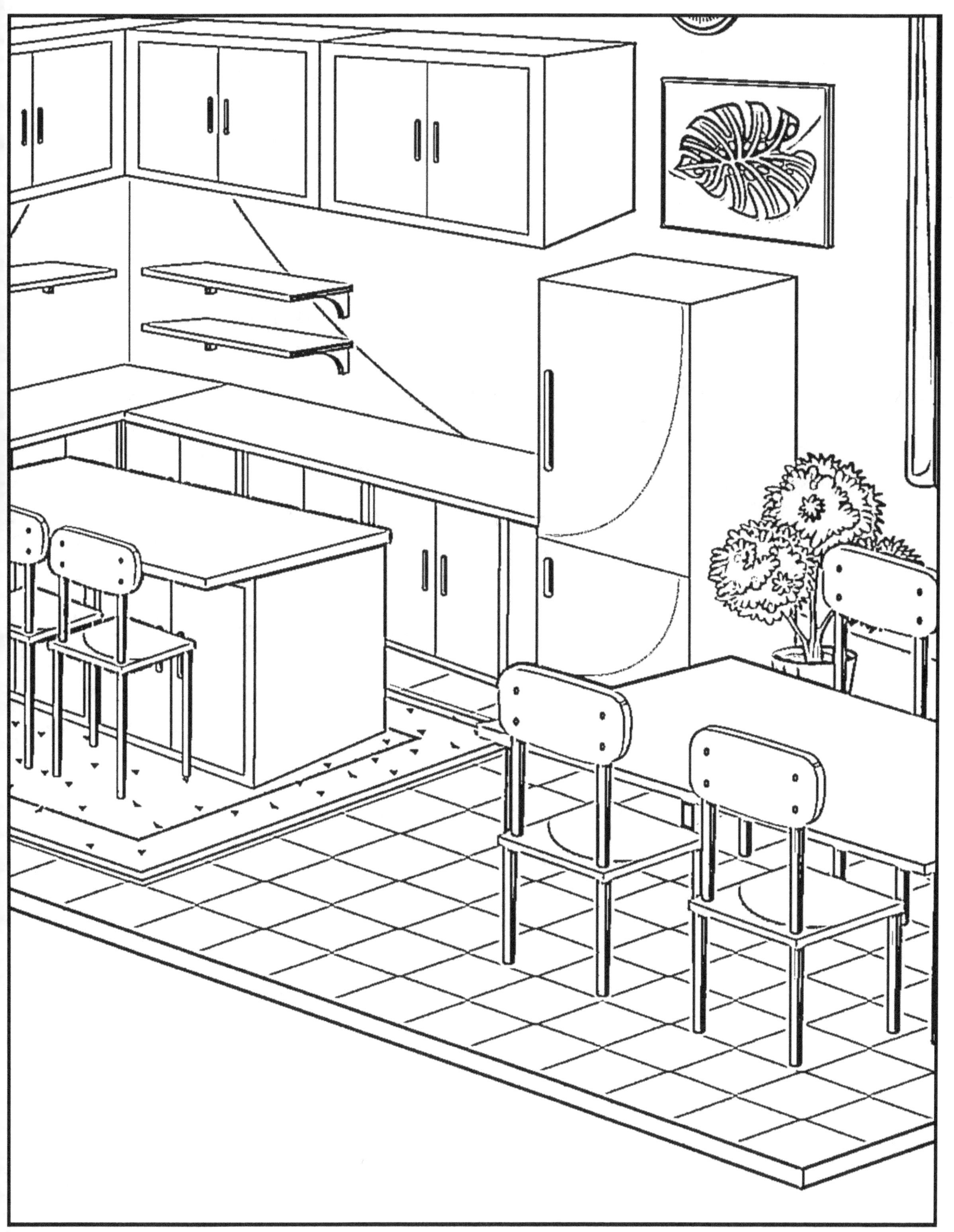

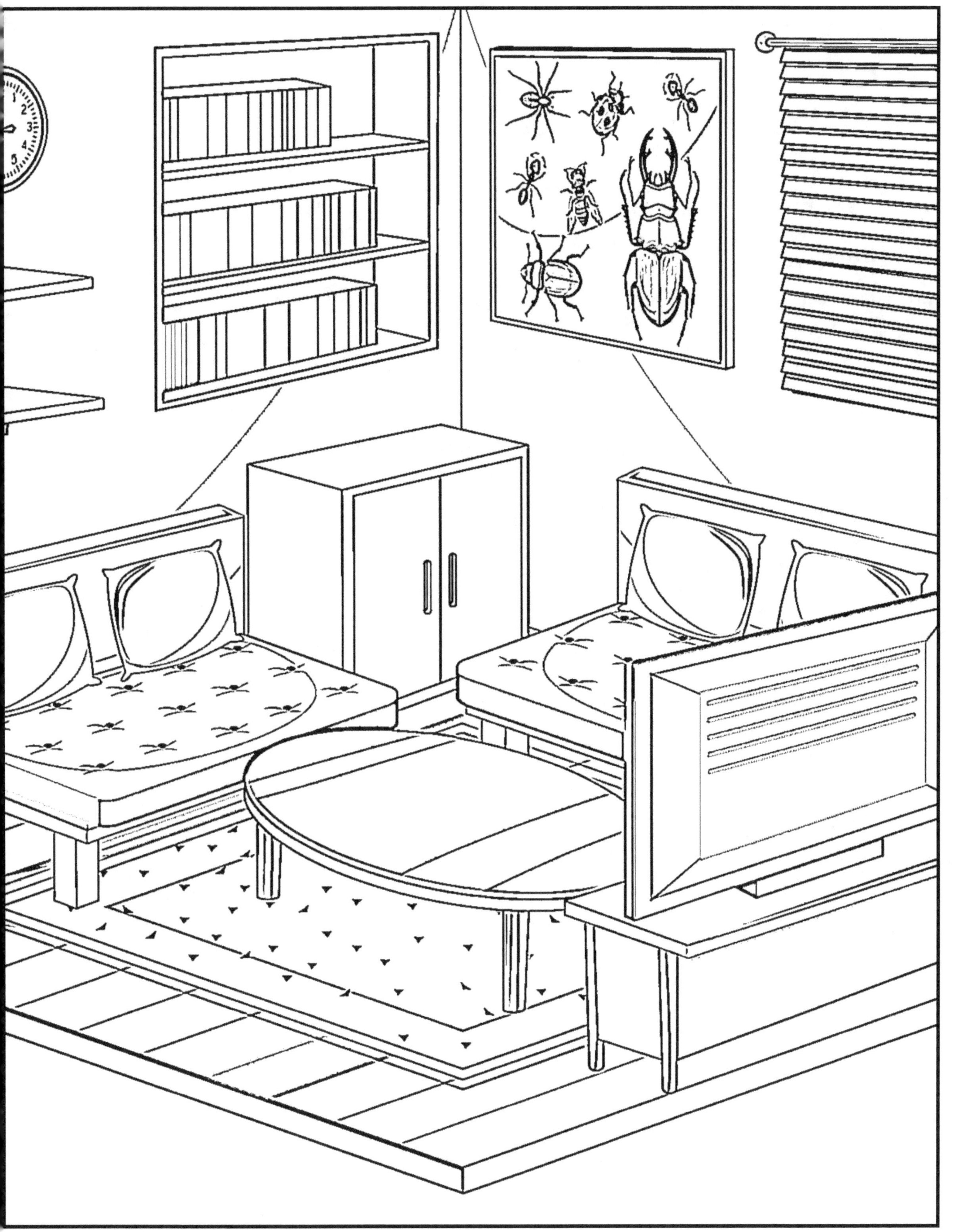

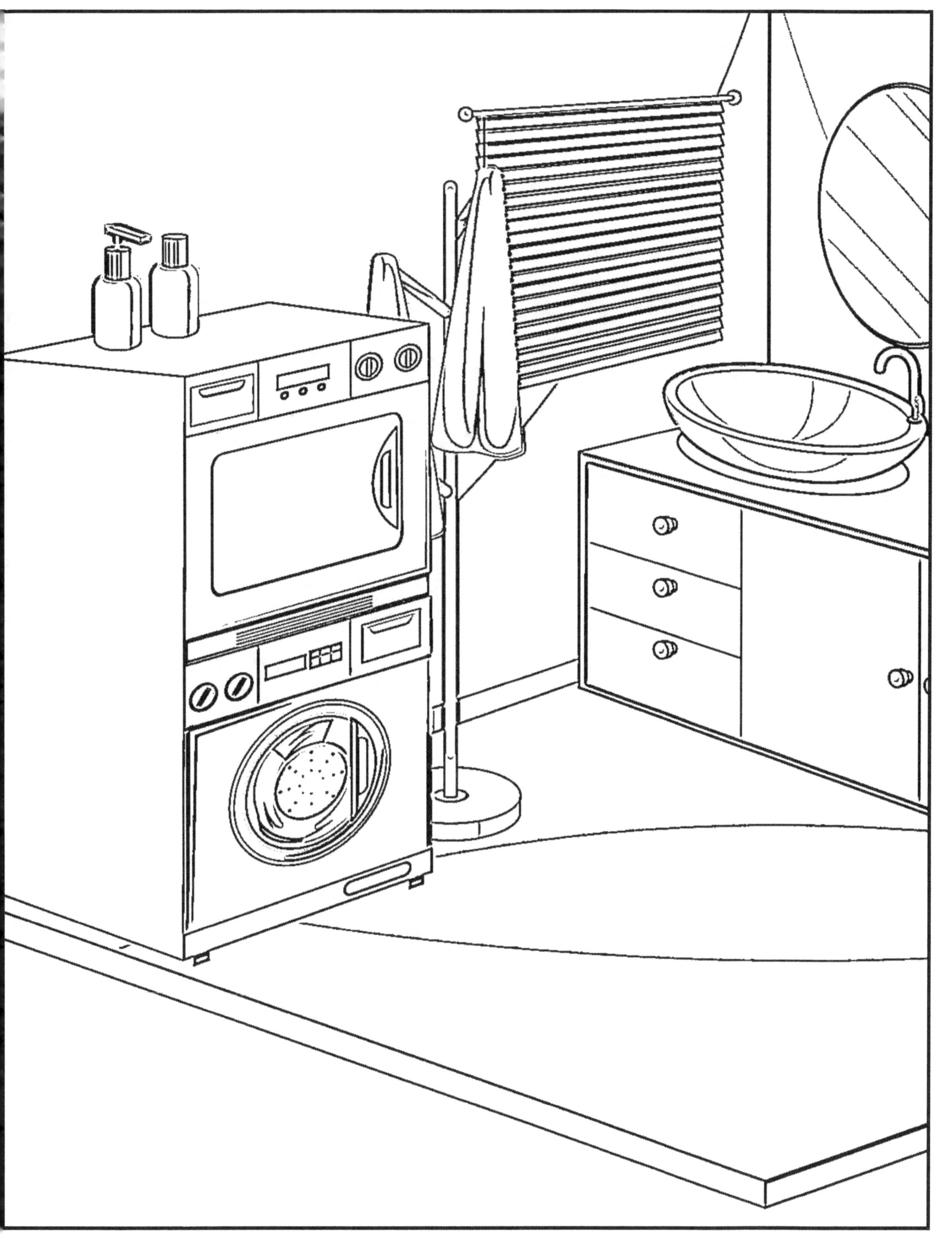

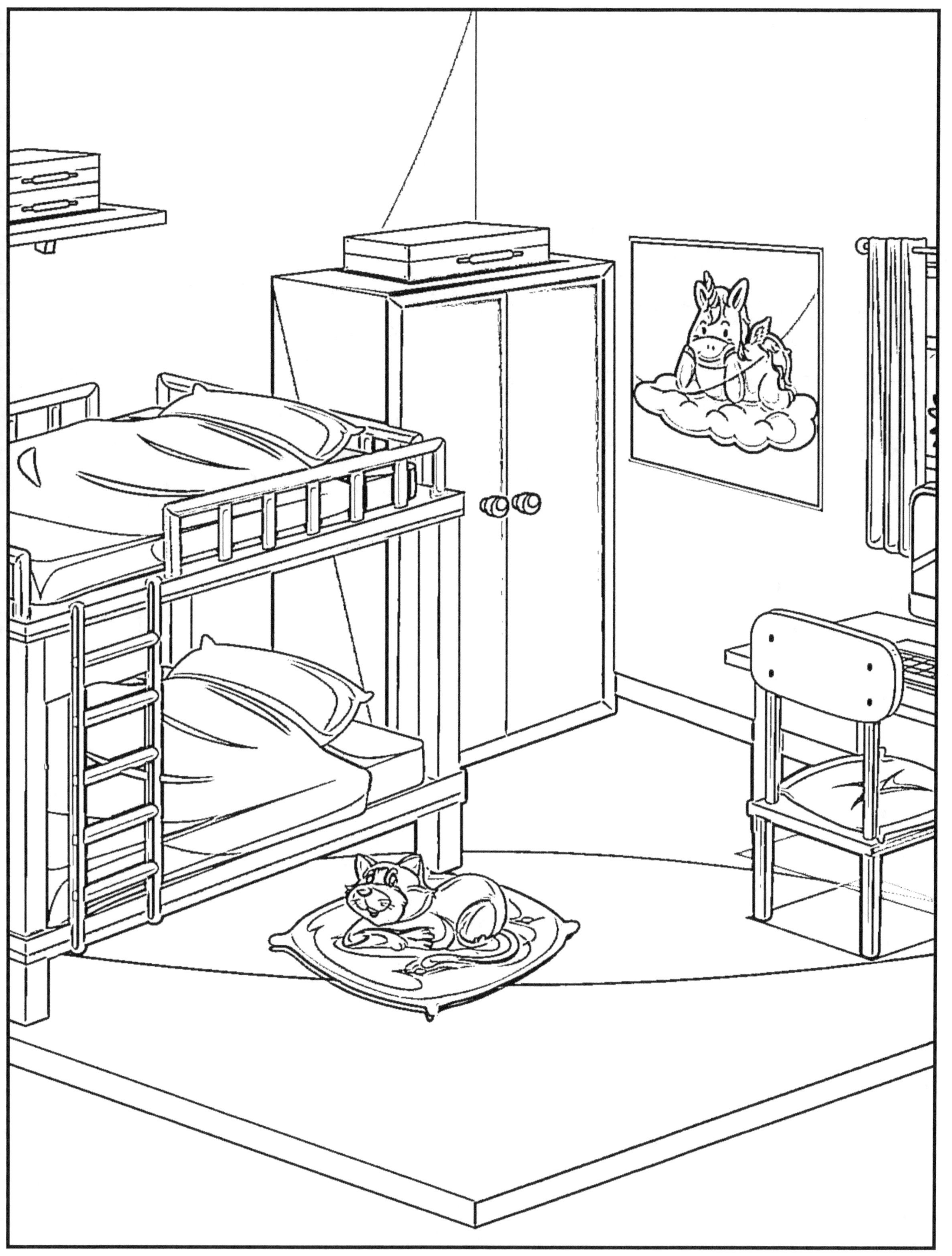

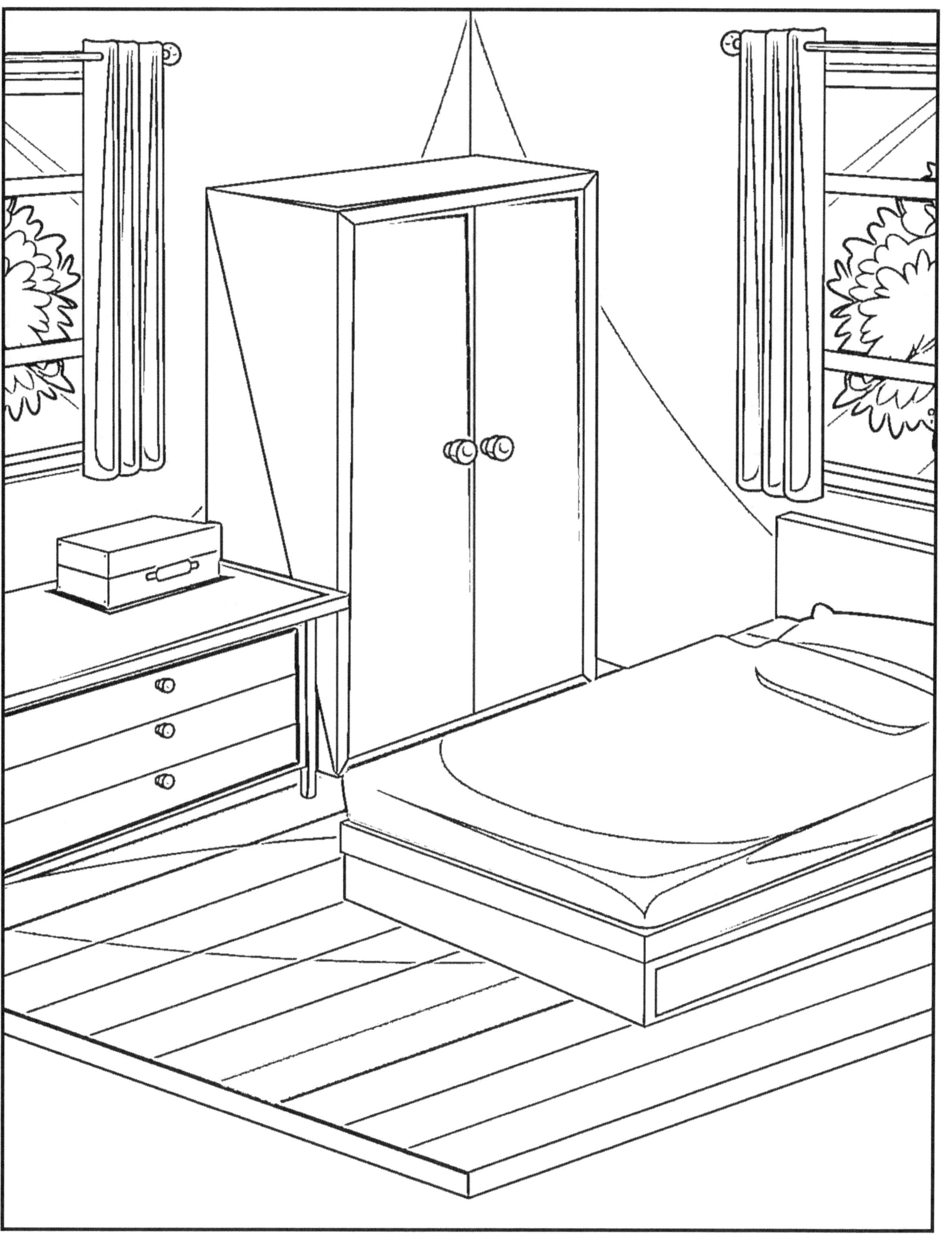

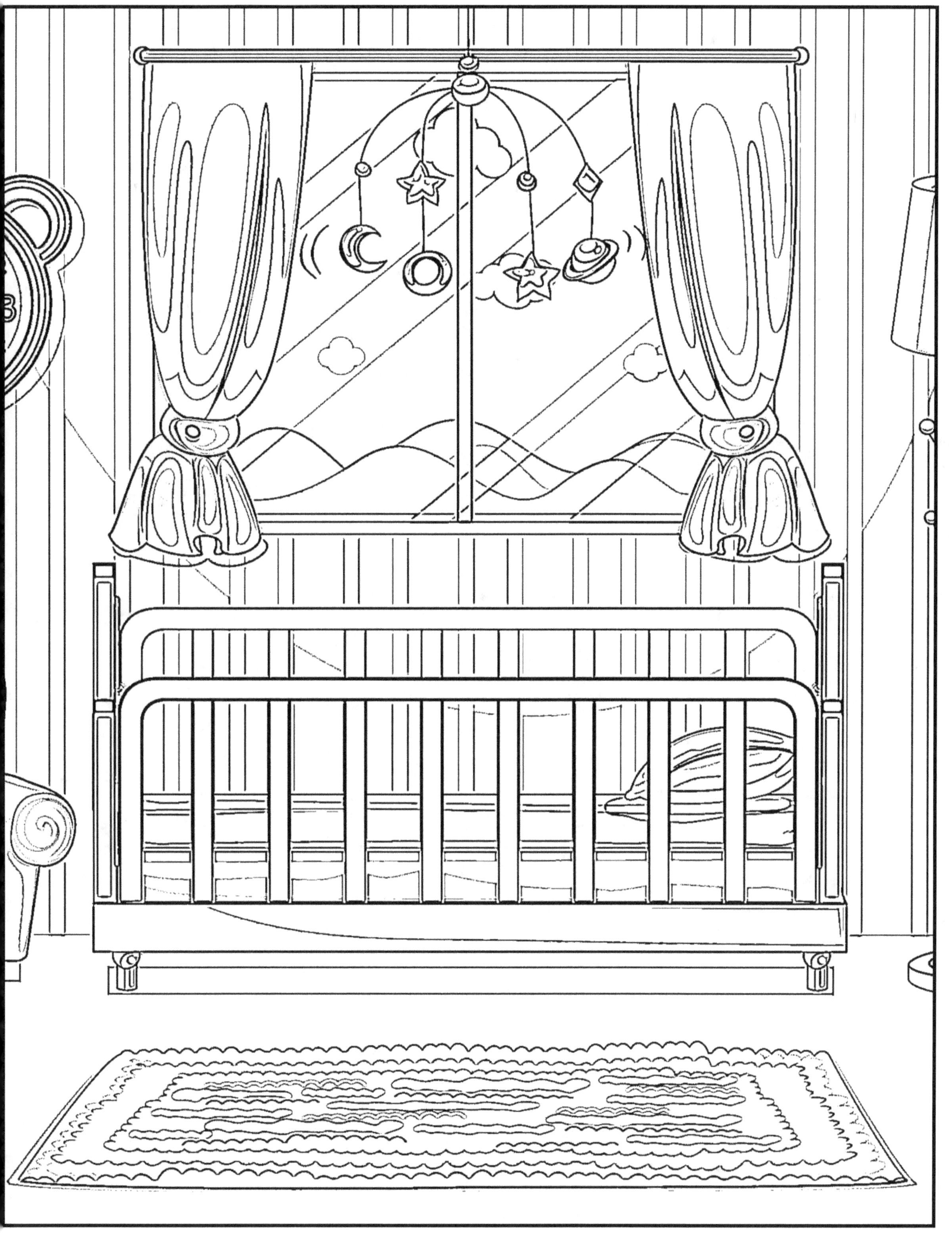

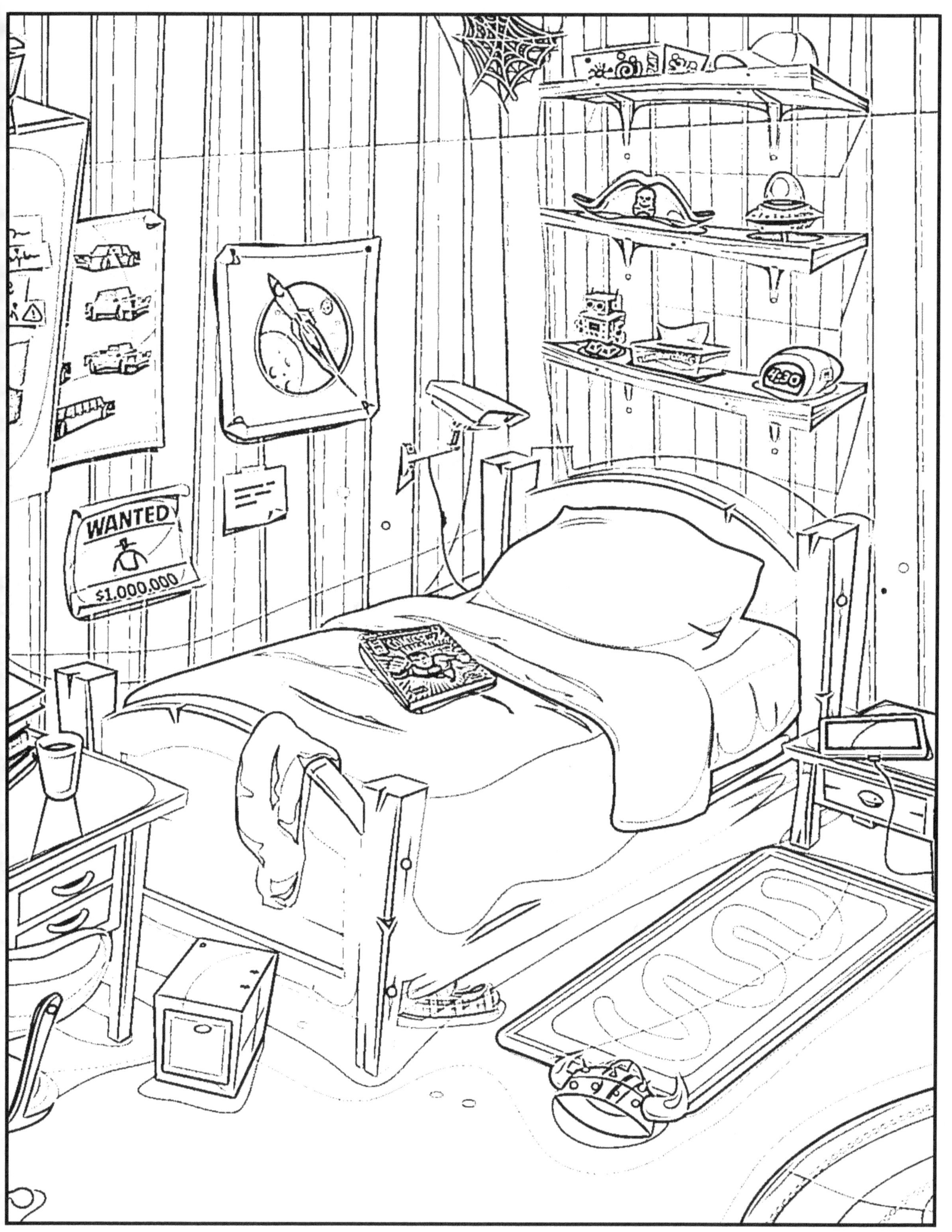

WANTED
$1.000.000

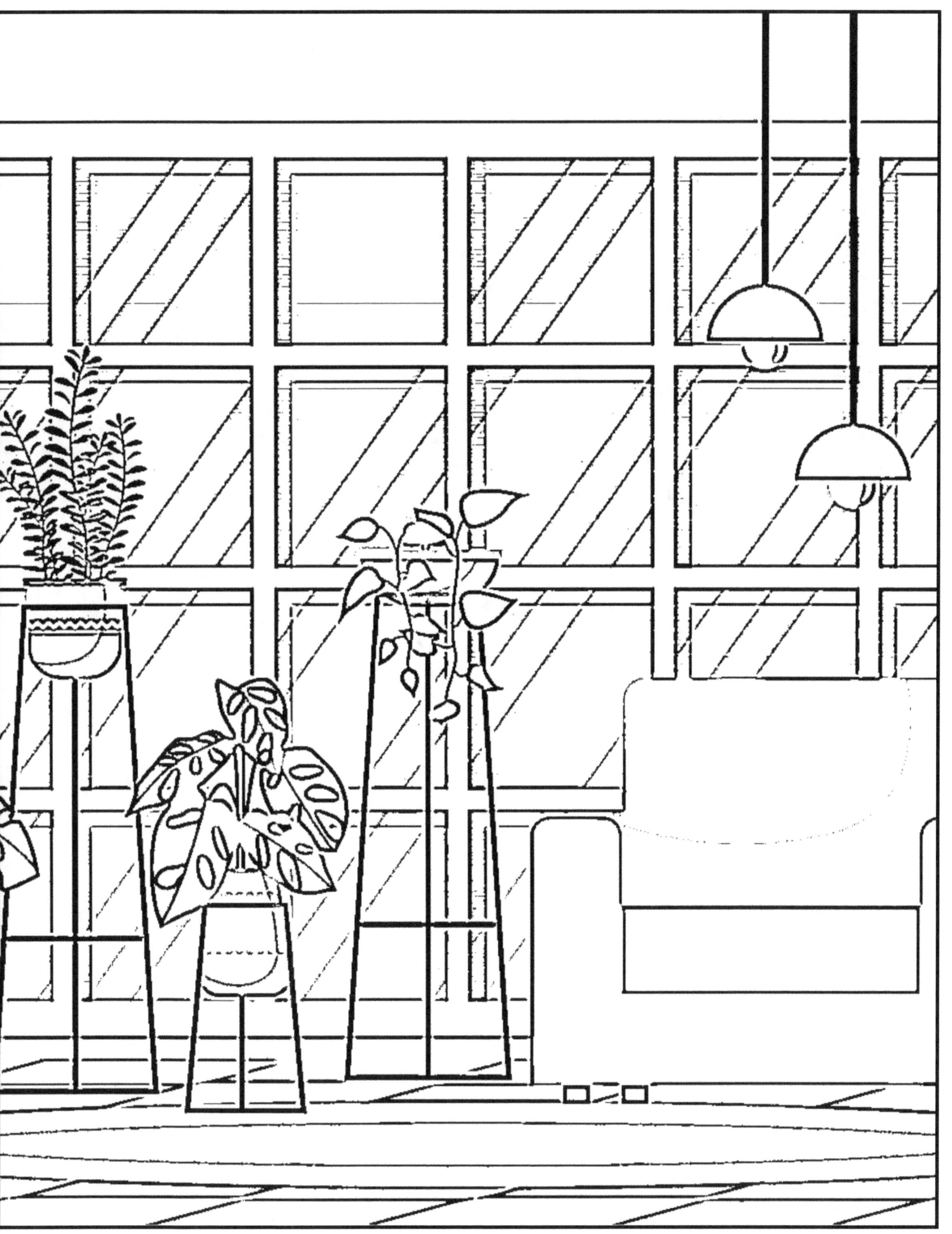

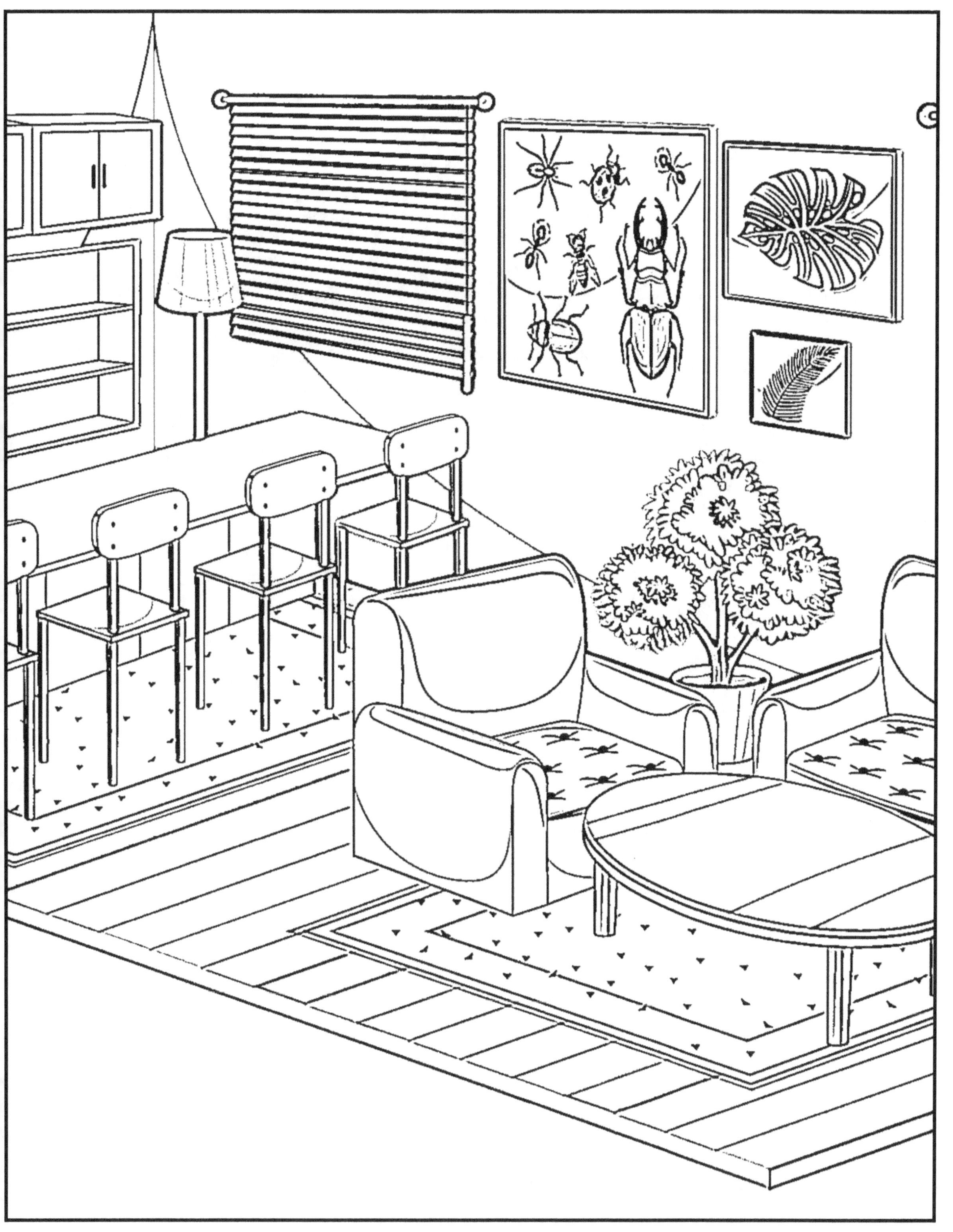

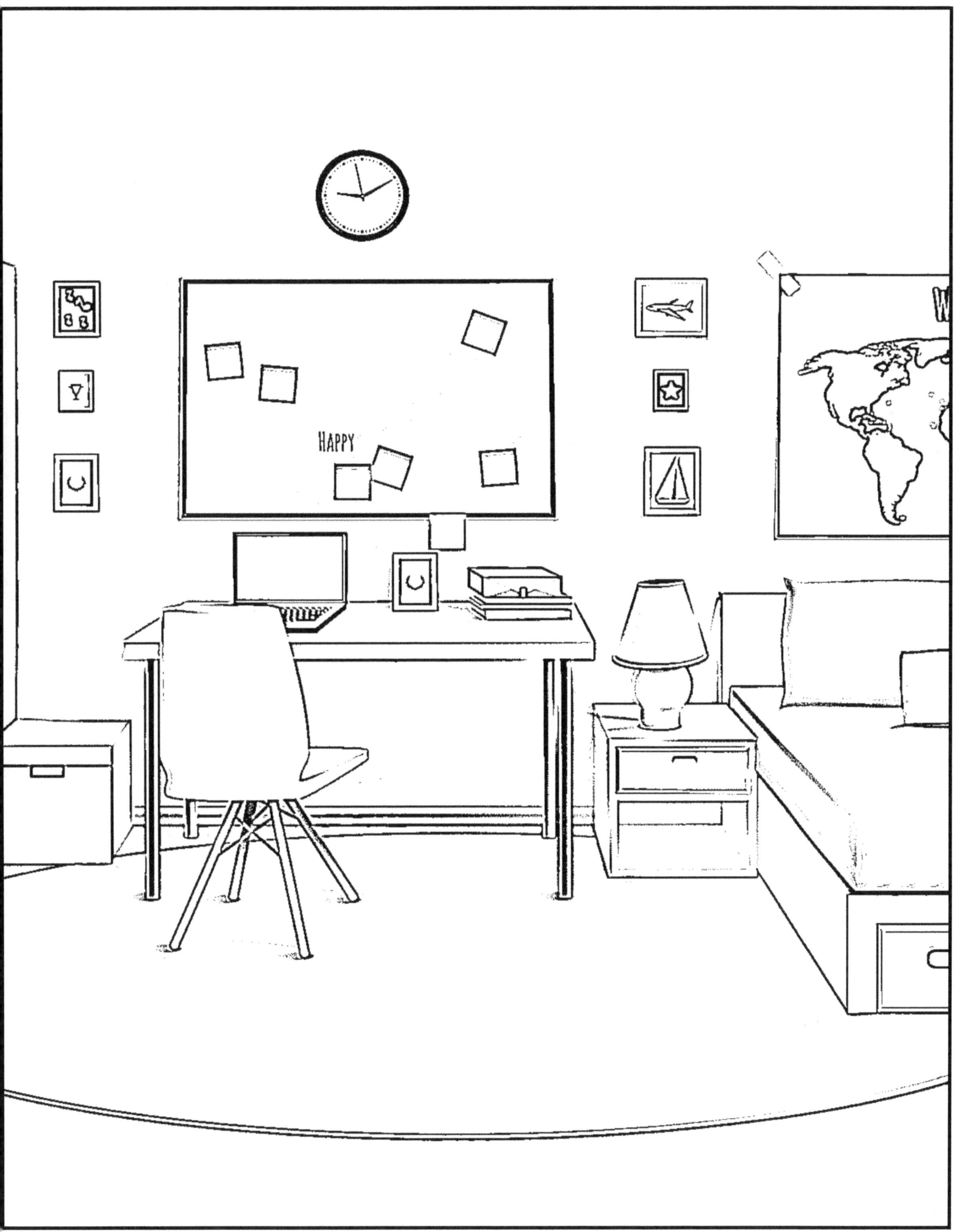
HAPPY

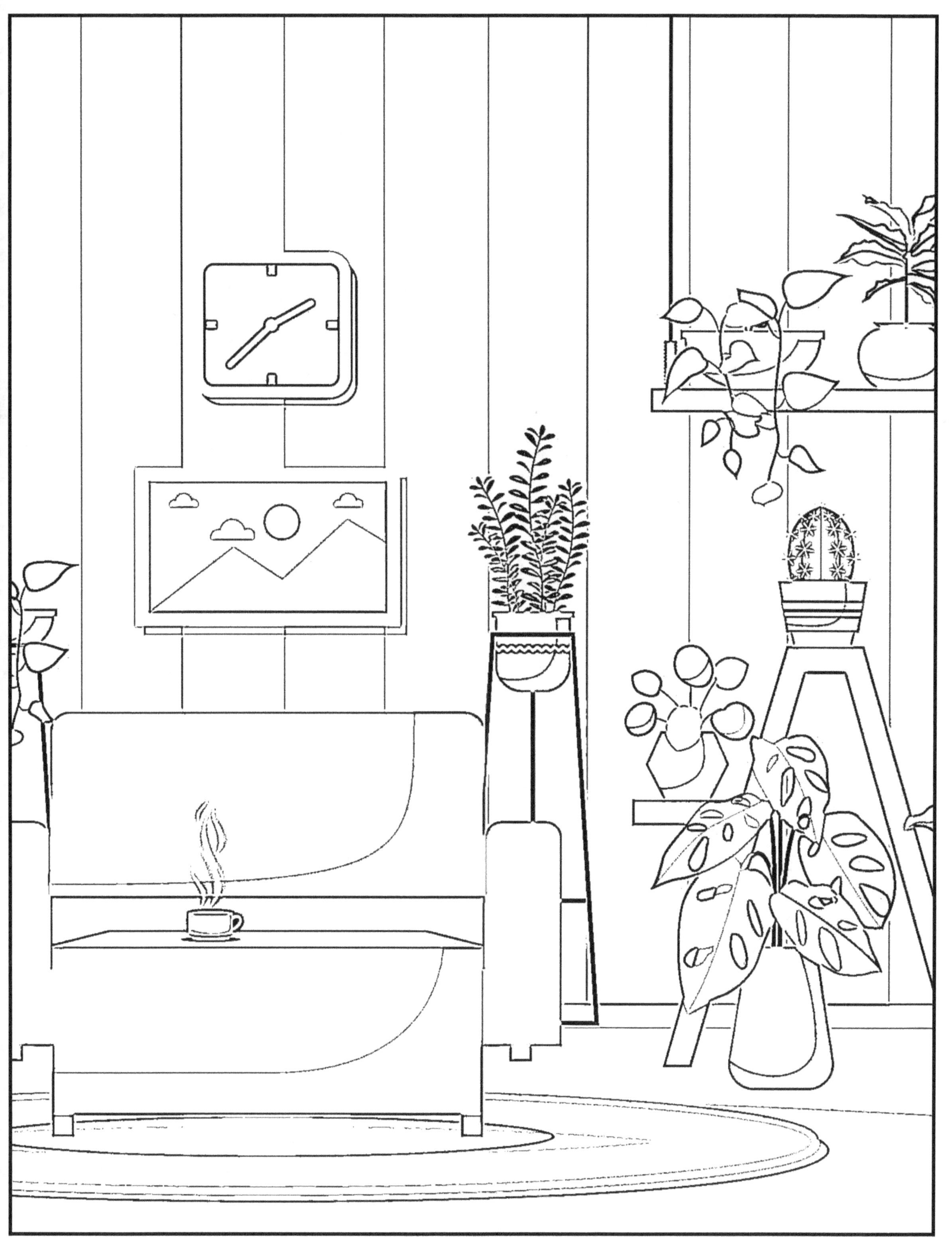

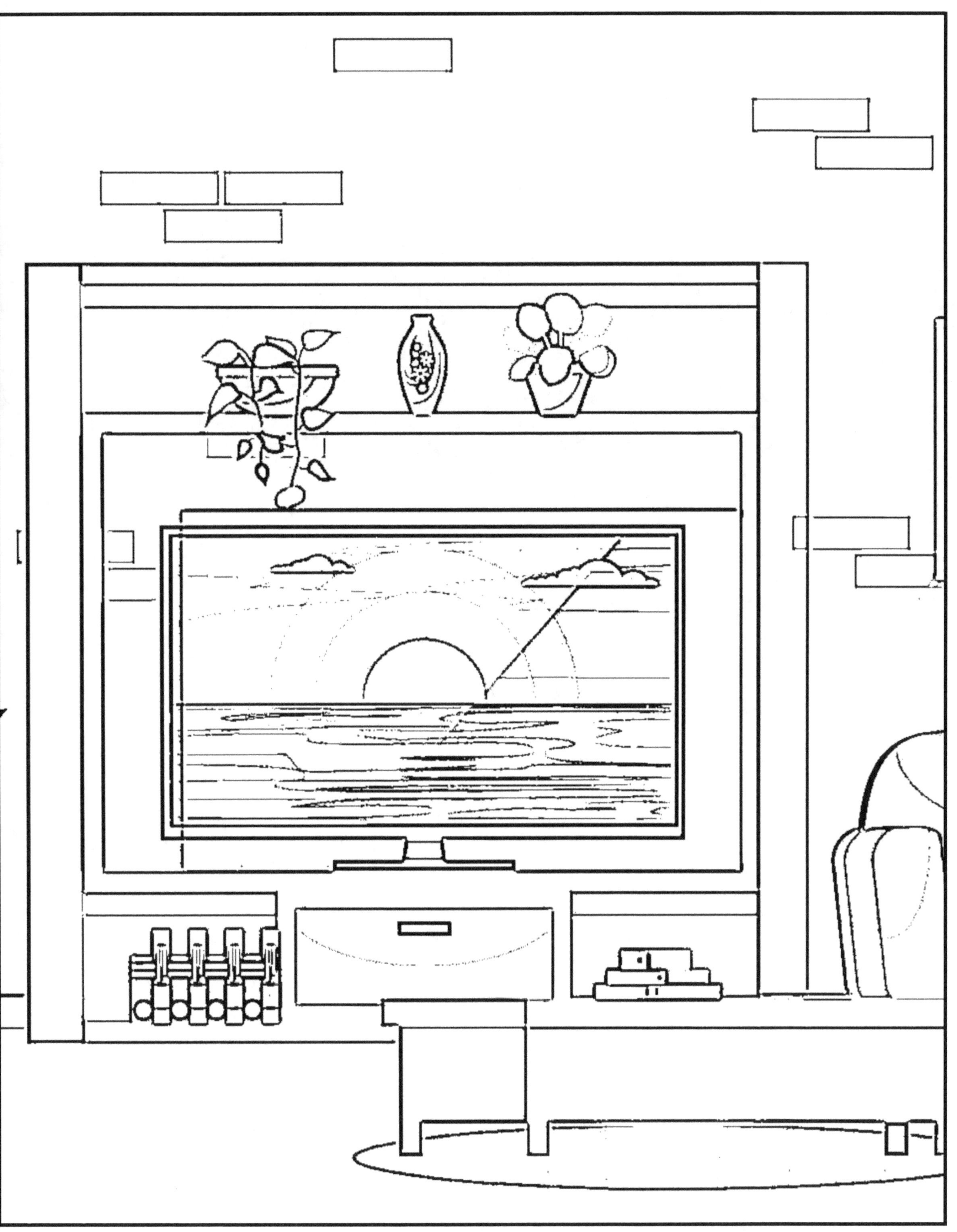

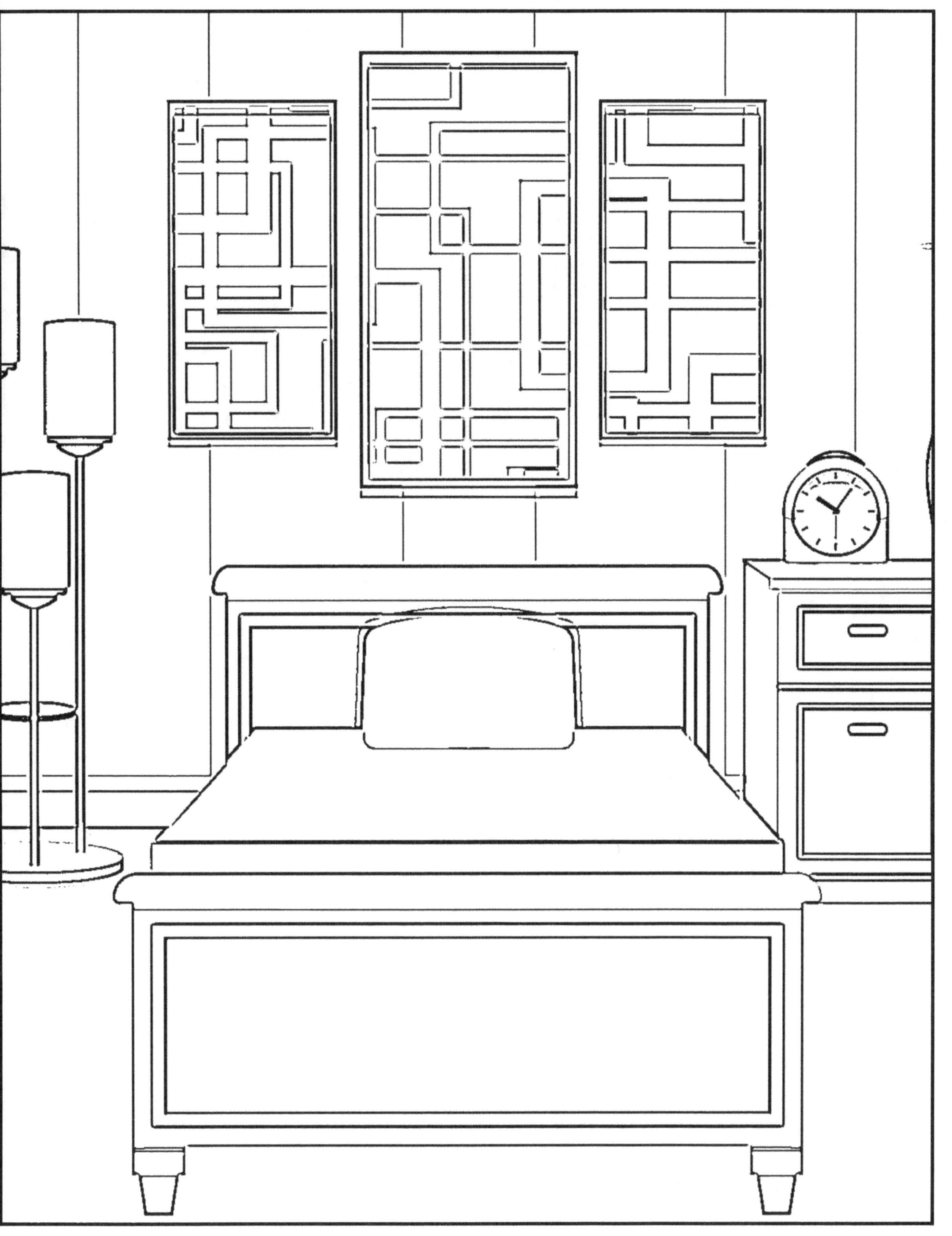

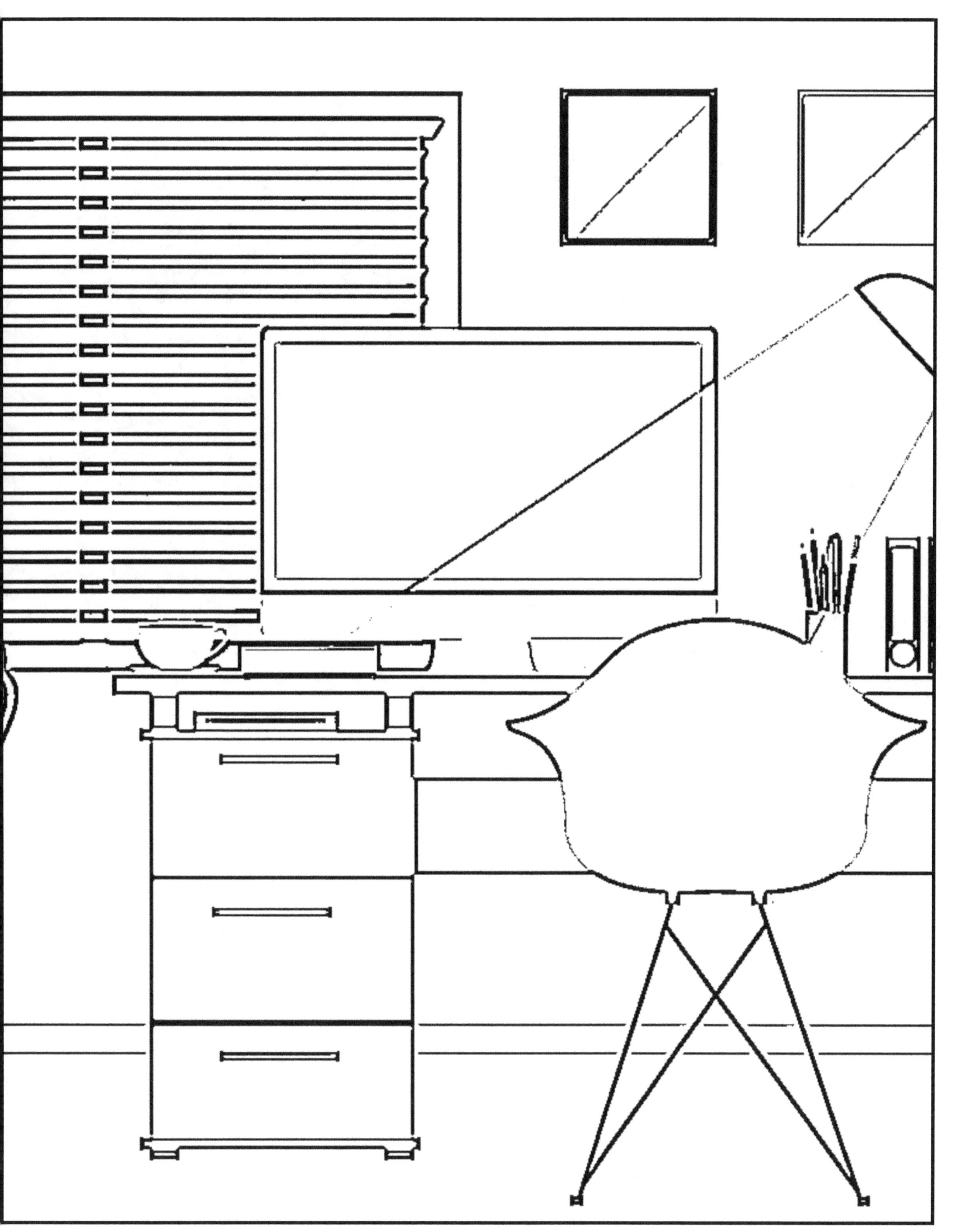

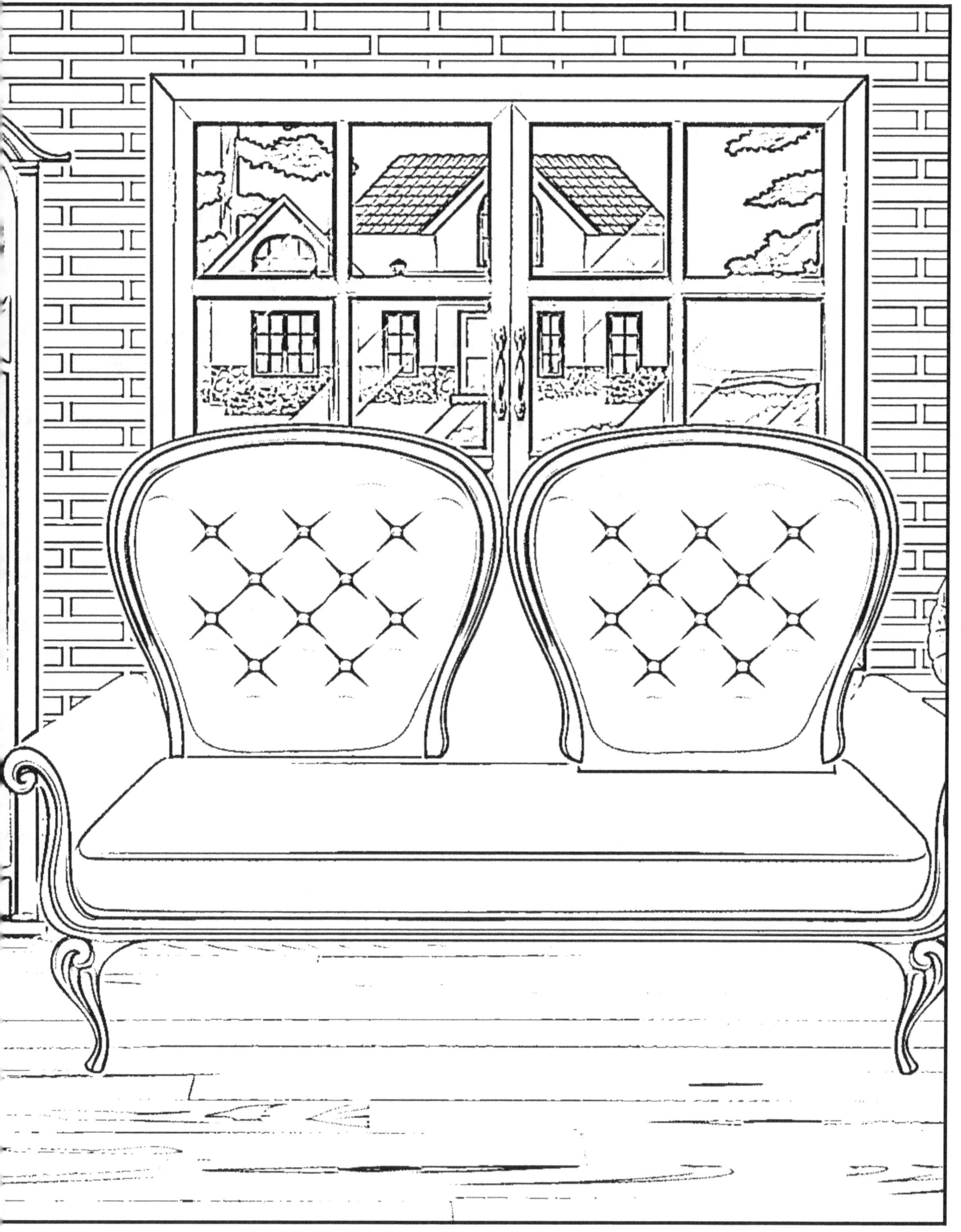

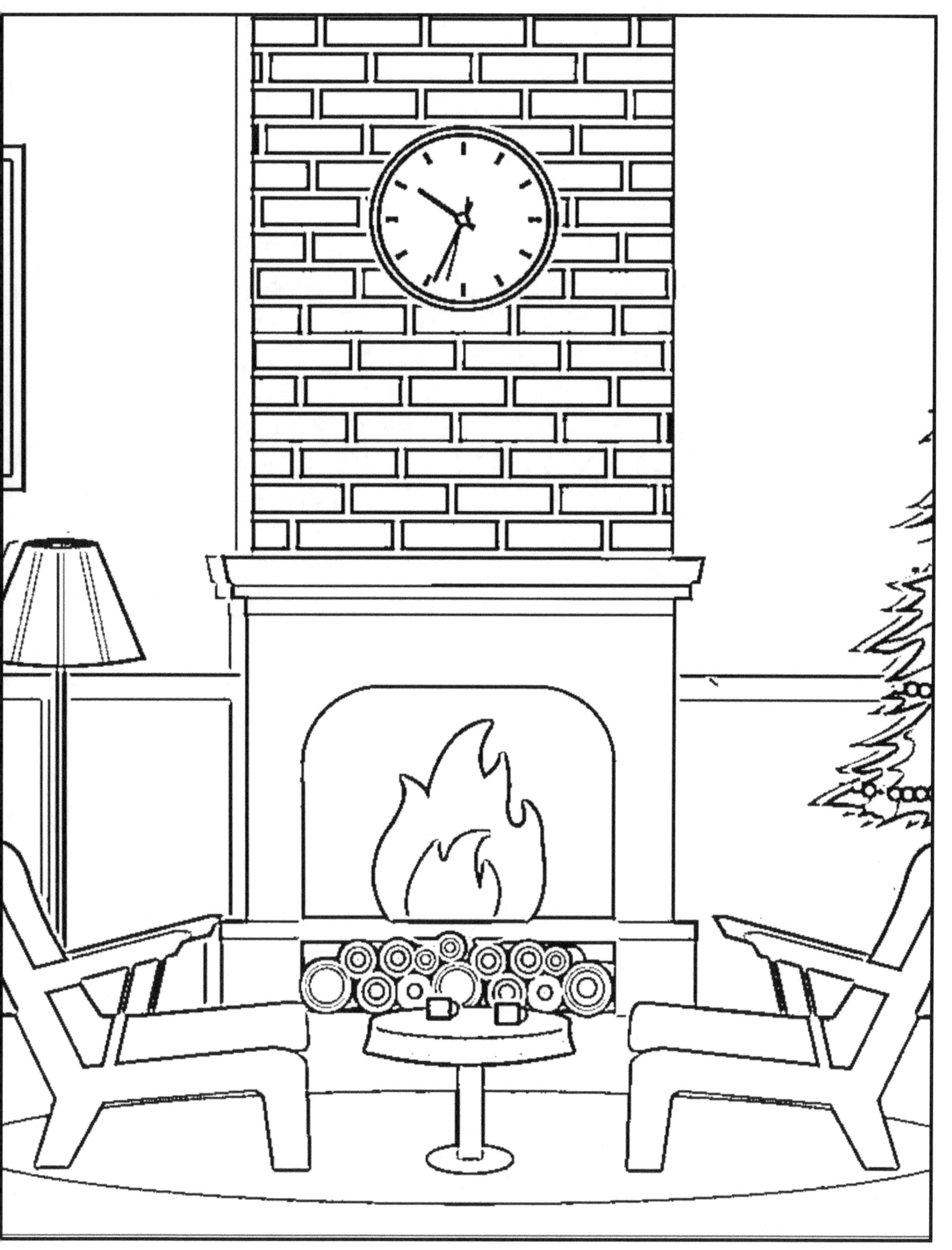

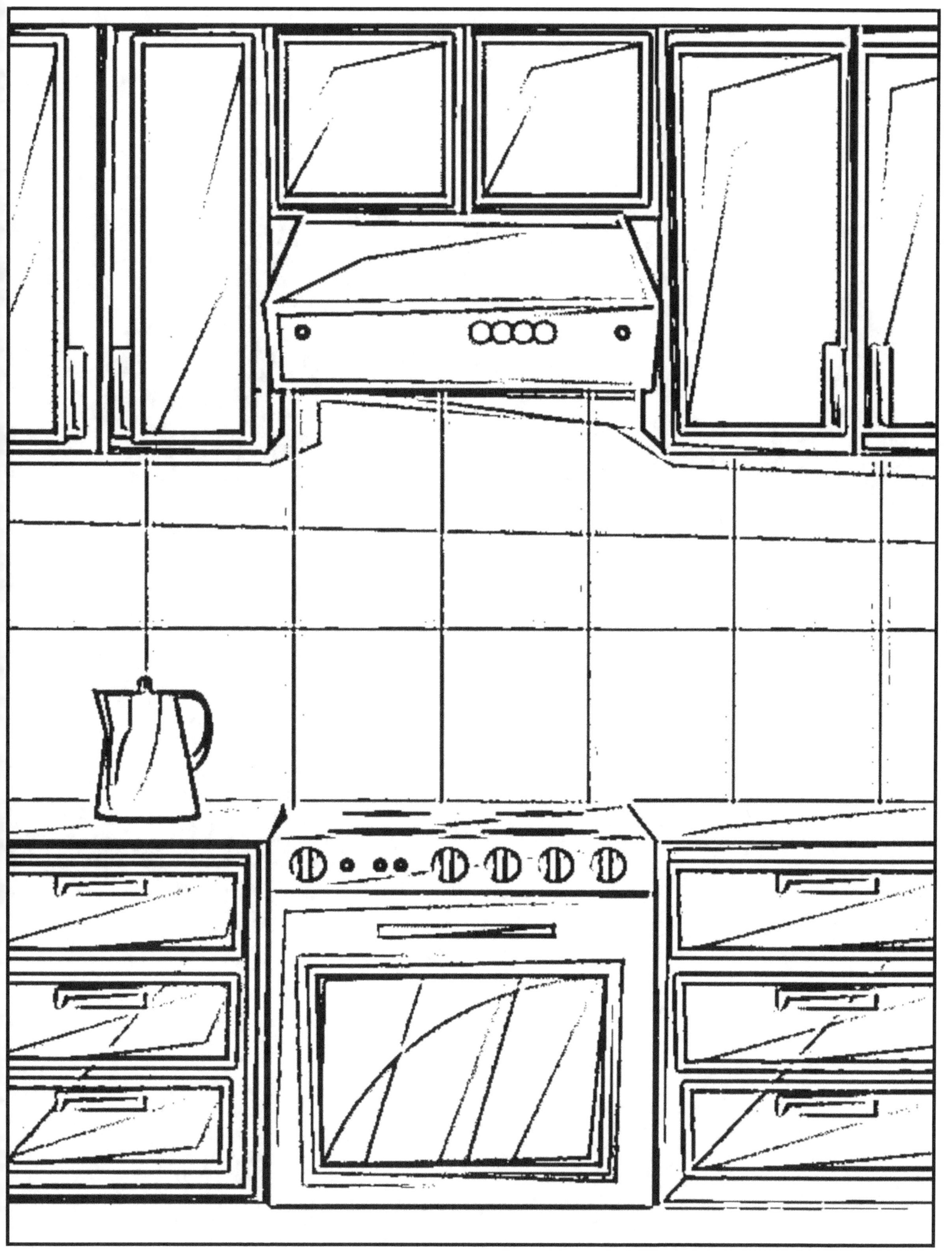

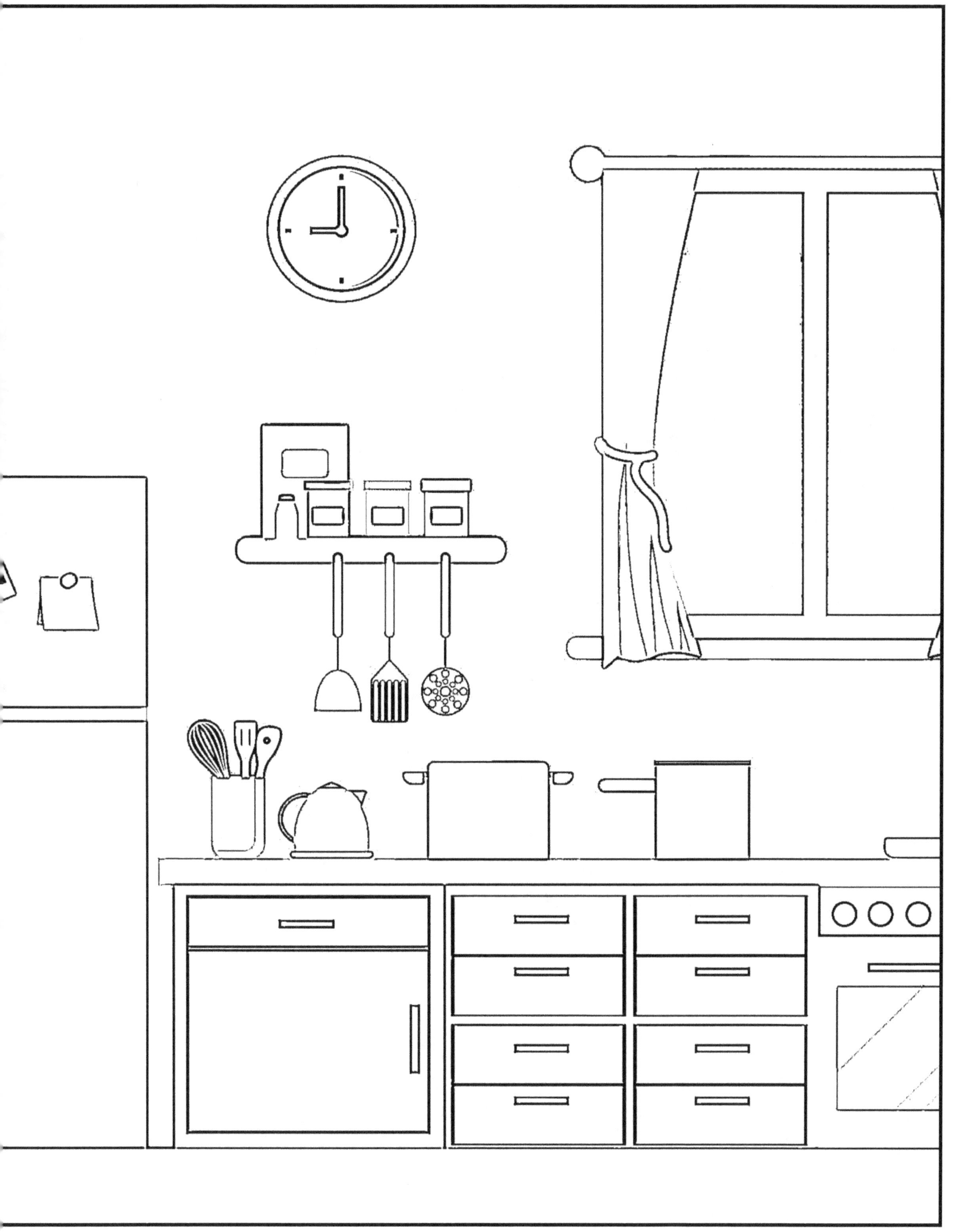

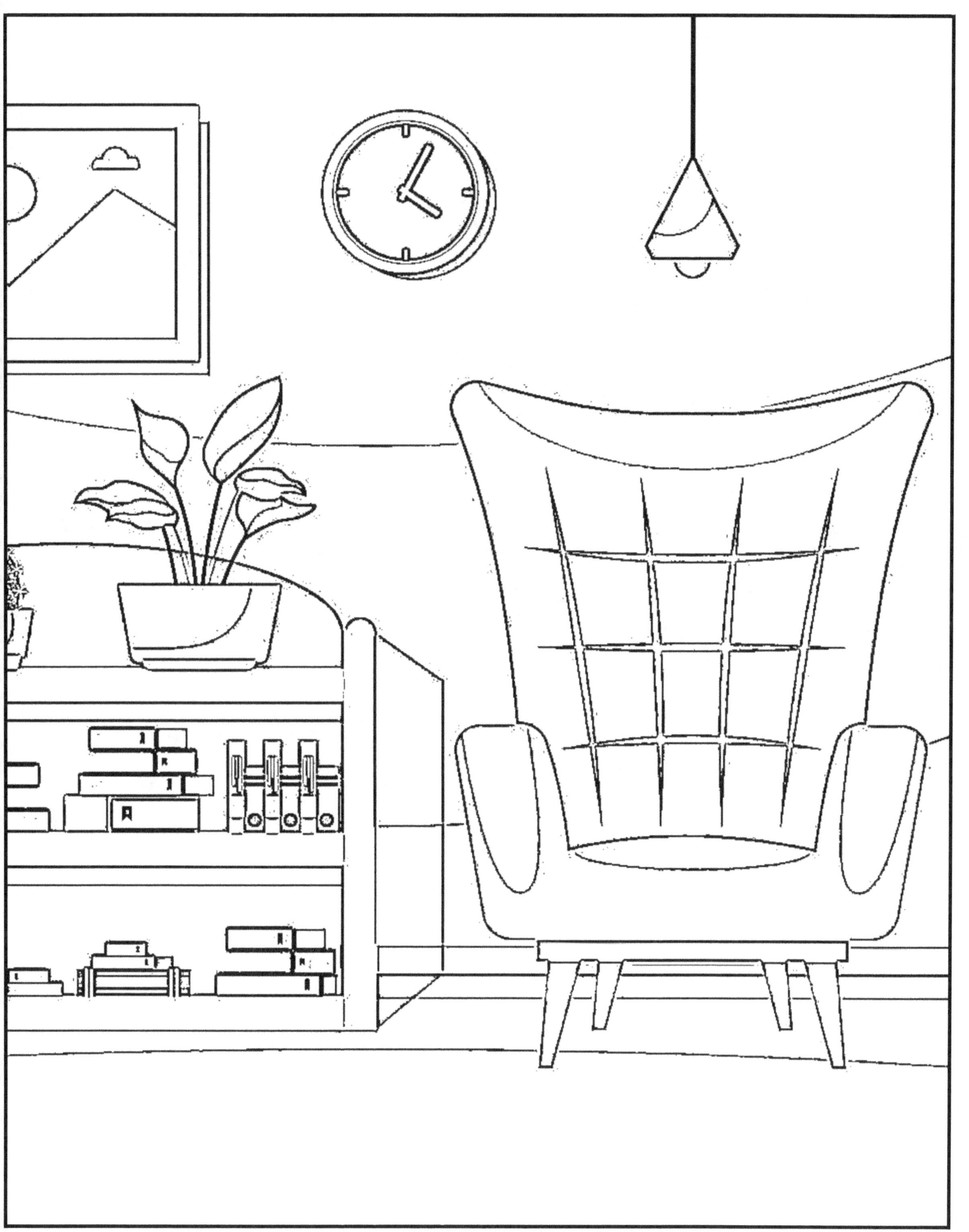

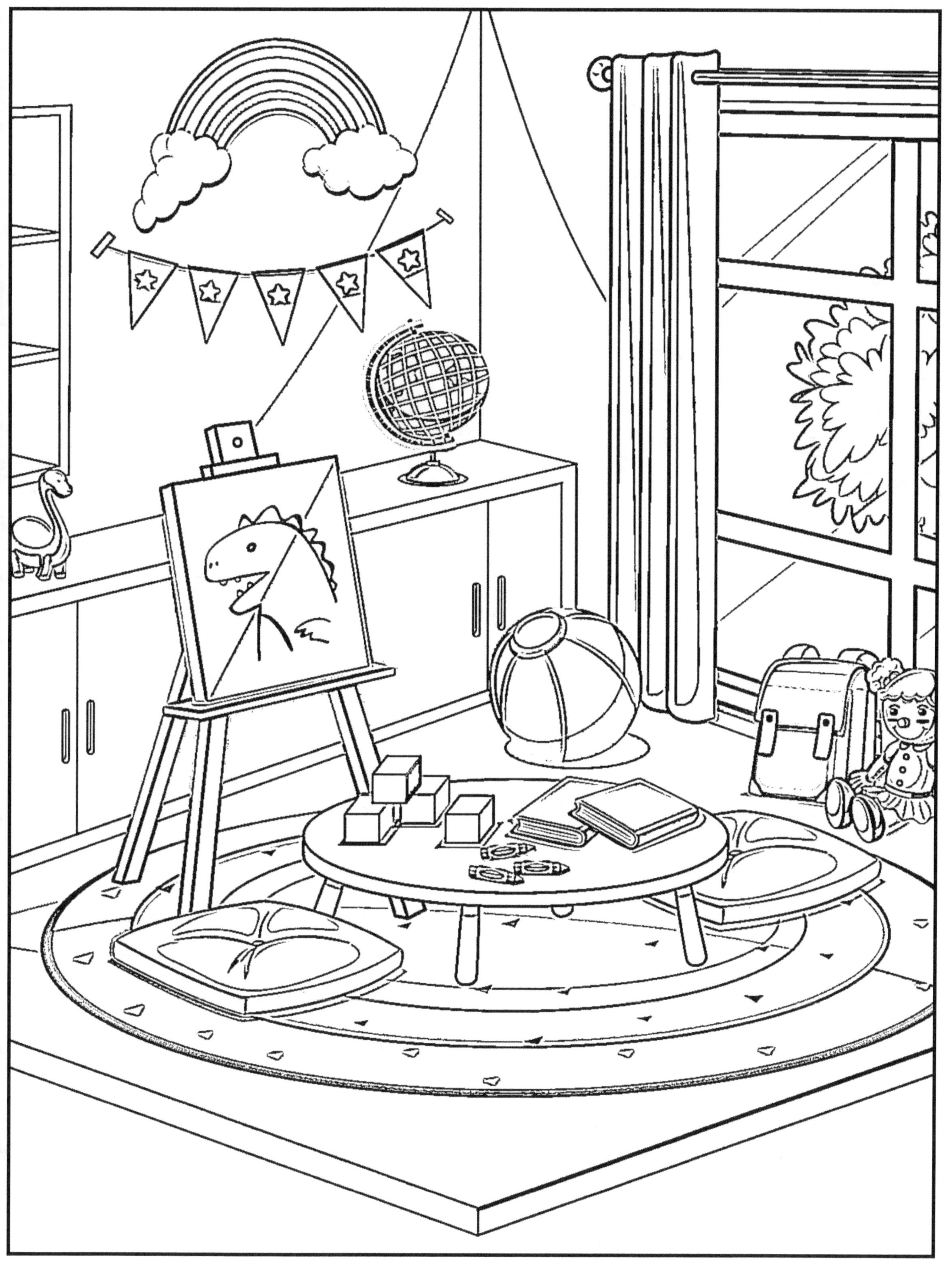

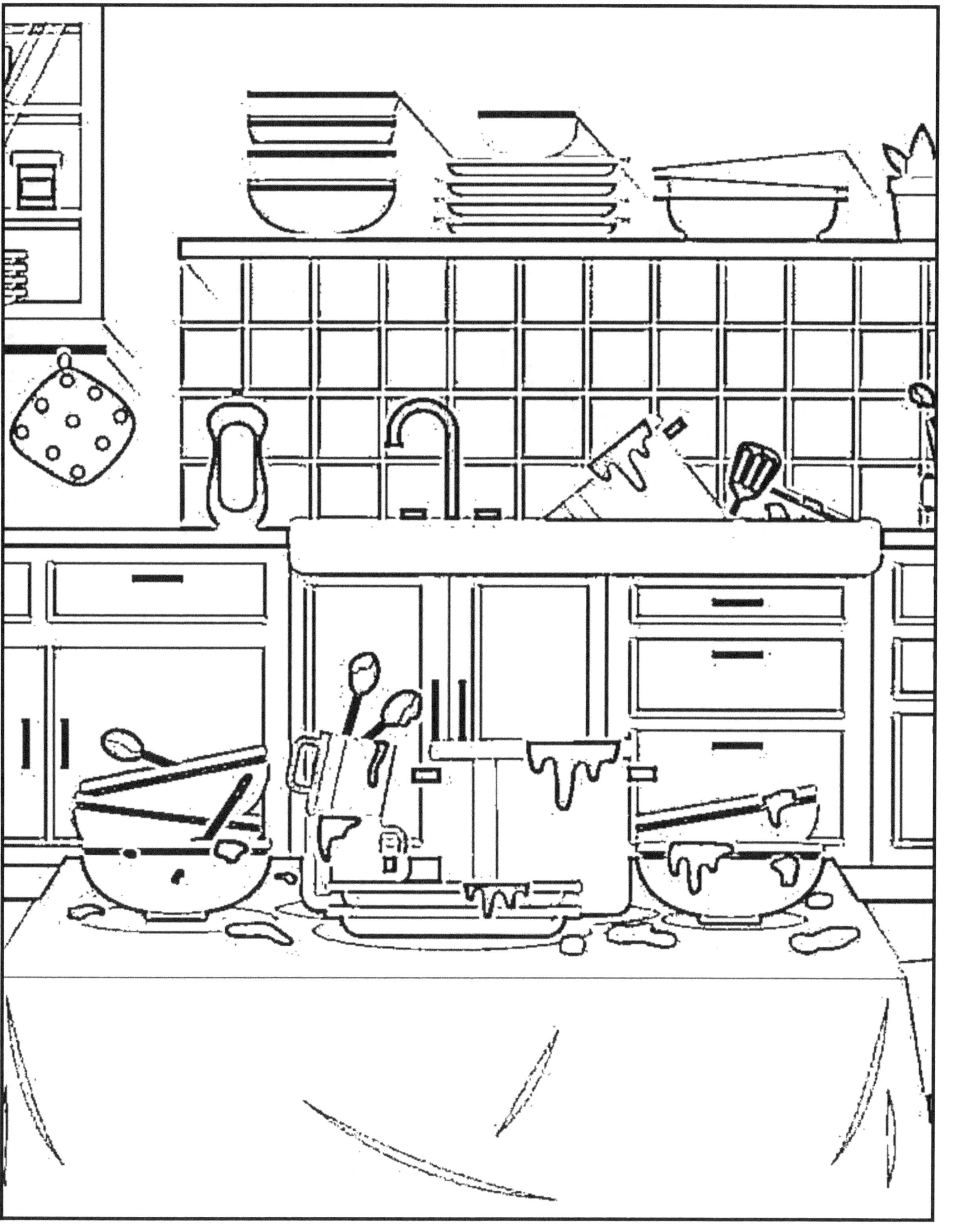

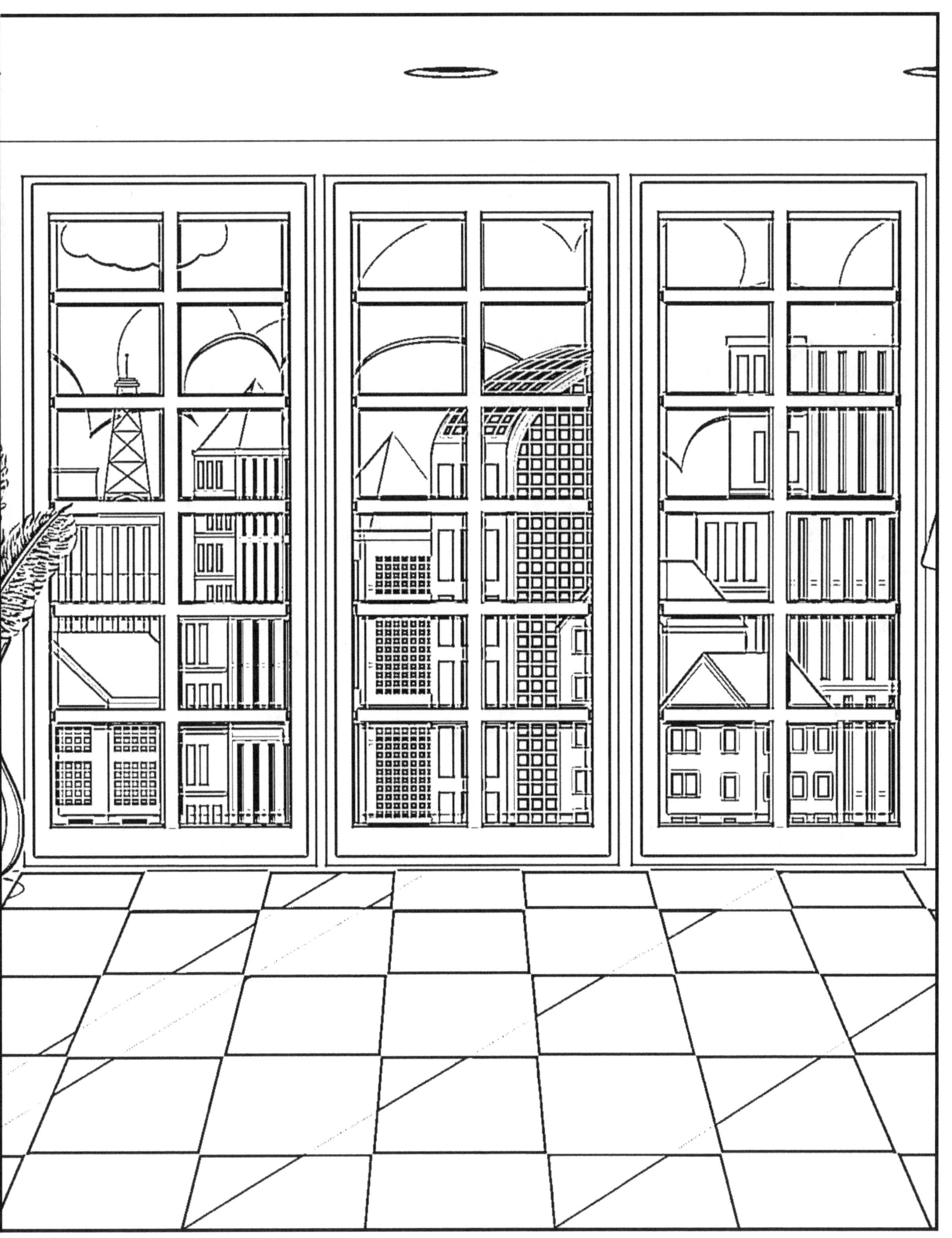